Dreams Wander On

Contemporary Poems of Death Awareness

Edited by Robert Epstein

MODERN ENGLISH TANKA PRESS
BALTIMORE, MARYLAND
2011

THE UNEXAMINED LIFE IS NOT WORTH LIVING.

SOCRATES

MODERN ENGLISH TANKA PRESS
P.O. Box 43717, Baltimore, Maryland 21236 USA
www.themetpress.com   publisher@themetpress.com

Dreams Wander On: Contemporary Poems of Death Awareness
Copyright 2011 by Robert Epstein

Front cover art, "Red Mountains," copyright 2010 by Ron Moss.
www.ronmoss.com   Used by permission.

Printed in the United States of America
2011

Dreams Wander On: Contemporary Poems of Death Awareness
edited by Robert Epstein

Published by Modern English Tanka Press
Baltimore, Maryland USA

ISBN 978-1-935398-24-0

DREAMS WANDER ON

LOVINGLY DEDICATED TO:

LOUISE AND MARTIN

AND

THEIR FAMILIES

CONTENTS

No one knows whether death, which people fear to be the greatest evil, may not be the greatest good.
     —Plato

If you stay in the center
and embrace death with your whole heart
you will endure forever.
     —Lao Tzu

All that live must die, passing through nature to eternity.
     —William Shakespeare

Death is not our shadow, it is our guide.
     —Gurumayi Chidvliasamanda

Death is a Dialogue between, the Spirit and the Dust.
     —Emily Dickinson

One approaches the journey's end. But the end is a goal, not a catastrophe.
     —George Sand

When death comes it is never our tenderness that we repent from, but our severity.
     —George Eliot

For 'Tis not in mere death that men die most.
     —Elizabeth Barrett Browning

Death does not extinguish the light. It puts out the lamp because the dawn has come.
     —Rabindranath Tagore

The angel of my affirmations (der Engel des Jasagens) turns a radiant face toward death. . . . I consider it my task to demonstrate that death constitutes part of the wealth of this formidable Everything of which life is perhaps the tiniest part . . .
     —Rainer Maria Rilke

The call of death is a call of love. Death can be sweet if we answer it in the affirmative, if we accept it as one of the great eternal forms of life and transformation.
   —Hermann Hesse

Man lives freely only by his readiness to die.
   —Mohandas K. Gandhi

The world is the mirror of myself dying.
   —Henry Miller

You never realize death until you realize love.
   —Katherine Butler Hathaway

After some years we will die. If we just think it is the end of our life, this will be the wrong understanding. But, on the other hand, if we think that we do not die, this is also wrong. We die, and we do not die. This is the right understanding.
   —Shunryu Suzuki

Perhaps the biggest obstacle anyone faces in the effort to understand death is that it's impossible for the unconscious mind to imagine an end to its own life.
   —Elisabeth Kübler-Ross

Death will be my final teaching, that is all I can know.
   —Roshi Joan Halifax

I know for sure that at the end, the playful stranger who appears is not death but love.
   —Kathleen Norris

We all pass never having spoken enough about death or about poetry.
   —vincent tripi

Preface

In Japan there is a time-honored tradition of writing a poem when on the verge of death. Originally, this practice was limited to Zen monks, samurai warriors, and nobility, but over time, writing death poems spread to the general population.

According to Yoel Hoffmann, a Buddhist scholar who compiled the only collection of Japanese death poems published in English, the chief purpose of the death poem was to bid farewell to life while conveying the essence of one's "spiritual legacy." (1)

Strictly speaking, the only true death poem, or jisei, as they are referred to in Japanese, is one that is written as one lays dying. By definition, jisei are poems written with consciousness that one's final breaths are numbered. Such poems contain an intensity or poignancy insofar as they constitute a keen grasp of life as it is about to expire.

In this collection there are only a couple of poems that were written on the verge of death. One of them is by the renowned American poet, Allen Ginsberg, who died of cancer in 1996. Although Ginsberg was born a Jew, he practiced Buddhism for many years. His death poem invokes an image of the sky, which the mind at peace is likened to when one realizes enlightenment.

To see Void vast infinite
look out the window
into the blue sky.

The other poet whose death poem is included here was William Higginson, a much-respected haijin, who contributed enormously to the development of contemporary haiku in the West. Thanks to Higginson's widow, poet Penny Harter, here are the last three poems Bill wrote (2):

smell of bile . . .
I wake to October
afterglow

October afterglow
will my lucky star
shine tonight?

hospital window
in the clear dawn sky
one full moon

The Japanese also recognize a poet's last poem as a kind of death poem.
That is to say, some poets die an untimely death and will have written a
last poem, which they most likely would not have identified as jisei.
While such poems may or may not have been written with awareness of
one's own mortality, they are nonetheless regarded as significant by virtue
of being the poet's last poem. This category of death poems are known
as zekku in Japanese. ayaz daryl nielsen, publisher of *bear creek haiku*,
identified the following as Dave Church's last poem before he died of a
heart attack (3):

LISTENING

by the window,
leaves ripple –
waves
being pulled ashore
at low tide.

Some Japanese poets chose to write their death poems while alive and
well. Regarding this third kind of death poem, the poet Jikku observed
(as quoted in JAPANESE DEATH POEMS):

> [T]here are men who prepare a death poem while still
> healthy. This may seem like exaggerated readiness, but
> fate plays tricks on us all, and we never know when it will
> ordain us to die.

The poems in the present collection may be regarded as an enlargement
of the third category, which I am calling death awareness poems—poems
written with awareness of one's own mortality explicitly in mind, though

not literally penned on the verge of death. These poems appear no less intense or vivid or poignant than those written as one takes his or her last breaths, and could just as readily be called "farewell" poems, I believe. (4)

Many poets appear to have meditated on the presence of death in the quiet corners and jutting edges of each moment. From one angle, perhaps it could be said that the Way of Haiku is to learn to fully live one's dying and to write from awareness of that place. What one realizes and records from the vantage point of his or her own mortality may bear a kindred spirit with Buddha, who insisted that the study of death was paramount:

Of all footprints
That of the elephant is supreme,
Of all mindfulness meditations
That on death is supreme.

The attentive reader may agree that there is something mindful holding the poems in this volume together. Perhaps there is a desire among poets East and West alike to leave behind something of enduring value to those who come after us. Despite life's impermanence, at least some of us want to be remembered not only for having lived, but for having contributed to humankind in some small, but significant way. Perhaps it is the heartfelt conviction that life is precious. Each and every moment of life is precious. These precious moments are quietly anointed by the poems contained in this volume.

NOTES

1. Yoel Hoffmann, compiler. JAPANESE DEATH POEMS. Vermont: Weatherhill, 1986.

2. Personal communication, January 24, 2010.

3. Personal communication, undated.

4. For better or worse, I have taken to calling the poems I sought "death awareness poems" rather than death poems in the traditional sense. These are haiku, senryu, or tanka written with awareness of one's own mortality, not someone else's. While I received a good many beautiful, touching poems about the deaths of others, I regarded these as outside the scope of the present collection; they deserve one of their own. Hence, my next project will be an anthology of poems on the subject of grief, loss and change.

Acknowledgments

I am very grateful to family and friends, who have provided encouragement during this project: Louise, Mel and Alyson Adler, Evelyn Epstein, Martin Epstein and Suzanne Kalten, Jay Schlesinger, Sophie Soltani, Kaho Sugi, and Miriam Wald. I also want to acknowledge my aunt Clara Knopfler, whose struggle to survive with her dear mother in the concentration camps during World War II, is recounted in her poignant memoir, I AM STILL HERE; the book is an enduring testament to the human spirit, and she is a source of great inspiration. I wish to thank Randy Brooks, Brenda Gannam, Linda Pilarski at Daily Haiga.org for granting permission to publish an'ya's haiga, Margaret Chula, Curtis Dunlap whose Tobacco Road blog helped to spread the word; and to John Dunphy, Dee Evetts, Alice Frampton, Ruth Franke, Lee Gurga for permission to publish Robert Spiess's poems; Carolyn Hall, Peggy Harter for permission to publish William Higginson's poems; Christopher Herold, Jim Kacian, Carole MacRury, Ron Moss, H. F. Noyes, George Swede, Tom Tolnay of Birch Brook Press, Michael Dylan Welch, and Liam Wilkinson. I am very grateful to Kathryn Anderson and Sue Villareal for permission to include their mother, Kay Anderson's tanka; to Marco Fraticelli of the *Haiku Canada Newsletter* for his assistance in locating Dr. Eric Amann and Marshall Hryciuk; to John Barlow at Snapshot Press for granting permission to reprint John Crook's poem; to Patrick Gallagher for granting permission to publish D. Claire Gallagher's poem; I am very grateful to Carolyn Lamb, who graciously granted permission to publish her mother, Elizabeth Searles Lamb's, poems which appear in this collection; and to Laurie Porad for permission to publish her mother, Francine's, poem. I am grateful to Peter London at HarperCollins for permission to publish Allen Ginsberg's death poem. Bruce Detrick's last poem appears courtesy of Joe Mondella and Bruce Detrick's estate. Thanks go to Father David Rogers for granting permission to publish Father Raymond Roselieip's poems. Charles

Trumbull generously offered his *Modern Haiku* database to locate poems related to the theme and has been very helpful in locating poets whose work I wished to include. Deep bows of appreciation go to the following poets for sharing their thoughts on the writing of death poems: Stanford M. Forrester, vincent tripi, and Karma Tenzing Wangchuk. Roberta Beary deserves special thanks for supporting the project from the beginning and for making thoughtful and constructive suggestions regarding the manuscript. I am indebted to Yoel Hoffmann, whose outstanding compilation, JAPANESE DEATH POEMS, which includes a brilliant introduction, served as a major source of inspiration for the current collection. I also wish to express my gratitude, once again, to Denis Garrison, publisher of the Modern English Tanka Press, with whom it has been a great honor and pleasure to work. Finally, I am eternally grateful to my partner, Stacy Taylor, whose support and keen editorial eye have been instrumental in making this project possible.

> Man never can plan fully to avoid
> What any hour may bring.
> —Horace

Introduction

There is no task as urgent for us as to learn daily how to die. . .
—Rainer Maria Rilke, LETTERS ON LIFE

Death is everywhere, and yet nowhere to be found.

If our own death must ultimately remain forever a mystery and its meaning ungraspable, how then can one say anything at all? While silence is one possible response to the enigma of one's own death, it is not the only one. In the West, where the notion of self has, to a considerable extent, replaced the notion of God as the source of meaning and salvation in life, anxiety frequently permeates the Western mind whenever thoughts of death arise (if at all). As such, death anxiety underscores the limitations of a self thrown into a world that appears indifferent to one's needs, projects, accumulations, and aspirations.

Despite the progress of science and technology in the West, the hopes and expectations of the eighteenth century Enlightenment have not come to fruition. Reason has not succeeded in eliminating any of society's ills: poverty and oppression, greed and corruption, war and aggression, disease and old age. For a period of time, it seemed as though science would render religious belief childish and naive. Yet, while major faiths like Judaism and Christianity may not have created panaceas for Westerners seeking guidance with regards to death, religion of course is far from defunct.

Still, among Western haiku poets writing about their own mortality, religion does not appear to figure prominently into the picture. It could be that contemporary haiku poets writing in the West have intentionally left out any trace of religious belief because it is regarded as a private matter or secondary to the haiku spirit. Then, again, for many in the West, religion has yielded to spirituality—a broader, less formal notion—that puts more emphasis on a sacred connection with Nature and others (human and non-human alike) than does the Judeo-Christian tradition.

But does a love of Nature lead to answers about one's place in the universe? about what happens when the individual dies? Walt Whitman, arguably our most American poet, unequivocally believed so. Hear what he declares in Song of Myself:

> I depart as air—I shake my white locks at the runaway sun;
> I effuse my flesh in eddies, and drift it in lacy jags.
>
> I bequeath myself to the dirt, to grow from the grass I love;
> If you want me again, look for me under your boot-soles.
>
> You will hardly know who I am, or what I mean;
> But I shall be good health to you nevertheless,
> And filter and fibre your blood.
>
> Failing to fetch me at first, keep encouraged;
> Missing me one place, search another;
> I stop somewhere, waiting for you.

Poet and novelist May Sarton intends to find her way back to the earth via the wind:

> I would like to believe when I die that I have given myself away like a tree that sews seed every spring and never counts the loss; because it is not loss, it is adding to future life. It is the tree's way of being. Strongly rooted perhaps, but spilling out its treasure on the wind.

If human beings are composed of the elements, as Whitman and Sarton suggest, then it would appear that, upon death, we return to Nature—to the earth, sea, and air. But is this knowledge in and of itself sufficient to allay anxiety or instill peace and serenity? For some, perhaps. But others will object that a love of Nature does not explain what happens to individual consciousness—the awareness that I exist as a separate and unique individual—when I die. Even if one does not subscribe to the idea of a soul which continues after death, the question remains: Is there life after the body dies?

More than a few poets contributing to this anthology have met this question with uncertainty. One poet went so far as to request that I manage the amount of philosophy that could seep into poems in order to allow enough space for this quality associated with mortality. Even those who have had close encounters with death, sometimes called near-death experiences, have not, in fact, died, so our uncertainty persists. In the final analysis, we do not and cannot know what happens to us after we die, and must live with this unknowing until the very end.

From a certain angle, haiku (and its related forms, senryu and tanka) are perfectly suited to communicate this quality of uncertainty. Insofar as haiku has been described as a form of wordless poetry, there is a tacit acknowledgment that whatever may be said or written about death is inherently tentative, provisional, and language is incapable of capturing that elusive something. Haiku, then, both point to and reflect the very uncertainty that characterizes death and does so by surrounding the theme with a rim of silence. In embodying the uncertainty associated with mortality, something transcendent appears to surface, however faintly.

Our everyday consciousness is a trance; I dare say that we typically walk through life hypnotized most of the time. Those who regard haiku writing as a "Way," a spiritual path, endeavor to awaken from the stupor of everyday living by beholding each moment as unique and whole unto itself. In effect, the haiku poet has unselfconsciously stumbled onto a means of dying psychologically, as it were, to the past. "Dying," remarks Elisabeth Kübler-Ross, the physician who opened up the domain of death and dying in the United States, "is something we human beings do continuously, not just at the end of our physical lives on this earth." When we become willing to die to the small deaths throughout our lives, time stops and new dimensions present themselves which are apprehended as one's intuition peers through a portal into the Eternal Now.

This is why the most subtly attuned poets offer up insights and revelations that startle and move the reader. Often the subject matter or setting seems utterly ordinary and commonplace. How on earth did the poet distill something so profound from something so mundane? In *breathmarks*, Gary Hotham, quoting T. S. Eliot, provides us with a glimpse into the workings of the attuned poet (which I reproduced elsewhere):

> When a poet's mind is perfectly equipped for its work, it is constantly amalgamating disparate experience; the ordinary man's experience is chaotic, irregular, fragmentary. The latter falls in love, or reads Spinoza, and these two experiences have nothing to do with each other or with the noise of the typewriter or the smell of cooking; in the mind of the poet these experiences are always forming new wholes.

When one realizes that life and death are not, in actuality, separate—that such separations exist only in the realm of thought—death is suddenly seen as part of a whole. The Austrian-born poet, Rainer Maria Rilke, couldn't have been more emphatic when he wrote in LETTERS ON LIFE:

> All of our true relations, all of our penetrating experiences reach through the *Whole*, through life and death; *we have to live in Both, be ultimately at home in both.* [italics in original]

Fear, anxiety, or dread may drop away at the moment when one comprehends the whole; or it may still persist, though perhaps in a somewhat muted form. In this connection, the reader might ask him or herself: Do you remember feeling fearful or anxious before birth? While this sounds like a ridiculous question, because one lacked consciousness before birth, the same may be no less true after death. Only those who believe in notions like karma or reincarnation may argue that consciousness does exist before birth and after death but, again, I would respond by contending that these are, at best, provocative concepts, suppositions which cannot be proved or disapproved on this side of life.

COMMON THEMES

Uncertainty

What, then, are some common themes that Western poets have discerned in the meditations on their own mortality? As previously mentioned, one key, recurring theme centers on uncertainty. Haiku writing provides a way by which to live with the uncertainty intrinsic to human existence.

Poets Ed Baker and Stanford M. Forrester, respectively, give voice to the uncertainty that travels everywhere with us like our shadow:

> full moon
>   here 66 years
> will I see you again

>   death poem—
>   what happens
>   if I don't write one

I don't think I'm alone in having observed that the more comfortable I become with uncertainty, the less frightened I feel about my own mortality. Of course, how I will react when in fact I die remains uncertain. We shall see. If I find myself terrified or overcome with sorrow as I take my last breaths (assuming I am awake and oriented), then so be it. As the Zen teacher Katigiri Roshi compassionately observes in YOU HAVE TO SAY SOMETHING:

> . . . we shouldn't have a particular idea of what a happy death is. One person is struggling and screaming in his or her last moment, another person is praying to God, another person is chanting the name of Buddha, another person is expressing anger and hatred. That is fine. Whatever a person does is fine.

The Buddhist teacher, Joan Halifax, couldn't agree more. The author of BEING WITH DYING had this to say when asked what she thought about "a good death": "I feel such aversion to the term 'death with dignity.' It's hype." Writer and critic Susan Sontag comments: "A fiction about soft or easy deaths is part of the mythology of most diseases that are not considered shameful or demeaning." How liberating it is to know that there is no "right" way to die. One may have wishes or preferences, but expecting or demanding that one die a "spiritual, peaceful, or dignified" death is unkind and unloving in the extreme. I will die as I die; to the extent I am conscious at all, I simply want to be with what is.

Such freedom opens the door to whatever happens; it also opens a window to light-heartedness or even humor. This is long overdue in regards to death and dying. While I have no particular interest or desire to paint a rose or clown's face on a garbage can, I also don't want to preclude the possibility of a light-hearted spirit surrounding one's final days. Pain may make this an unlikely prospect, but even in the throes of unbearable pain, one might very well grasp the absurdity of it all and blurt out some inanity that cracks one up and those around one. Something akin to this happened when I read following dialogue between the Zen master Hakuin and a nobleman quoted in THE ART OF DYING:

'What happens to an enlightened man at death?'
'Why ask me?'
'Because you are a Zen master.'
'Yes, but not a dead one.'

Death Dreams

In the nocturnal world of dreams, our unconscious endeavors to work out what the conscious self cannot. Death is one of the themes that can recur in dreams; some of these death dreams are so harrowing that they may be vividly recalled years later; others disappear so quickly upon awakening that one may have completely "forgotten" the dream by the time he or she sits down with a cup of coffee. (Freud called this repression.)

Although I collected about 500 poems related to death awareness, only one poem by Bill Higginson specifically approaches death from the vantage point of dreams and hints at anticipatory grief. The poet's anxiety about death is both palpable and poignant.

death dream . . .
I struggle awake to the cry
of a mourning dove

Dying

Death is an instant in time—no different, in this respect, from any other moment—yet of course it is also momentous; everything we have been ceases. But death is preceded by a process of dying, the details of which are the subject of many poets' attention. Dying is treated as worthy a topic as death is and no less significant.

Insofar as science and medicine have prolonged the life span of modern day poets, it is often the diagnosis of a terminal illness, rather than the conquest of triumphant warlords, which presages dying. And so more than a few poets find themselves writing about their first brush with death, as does Marian Olson:

diagnosis
spring sweeter
because of it

The practical realist is not invariably undone by the dissolution of everything with death. Diligence must be brought to bear even in dying—perhaps as a means of managing anxiety—and so Carmie Stoifer goes about her business:

preparing for
my death
I sort the bills

Still, even putting one's papers in order can be messy. Carmel Lively Westerman hints at the acrimony or avarice that, sadly, can all too often be triggered by a parent's death:

dental gold—
I will it to my son

Time

Central to death is our relation to time. While most people in their daily lives relegate death to the basement or the back of the closet, time cannot be so easily banished. On the contrary, most of us living harried, modern lives are preoccupied, if not persecuted, by the passage of time. There are many platitudes that people share with one another, almost on a daily basis, which reinforce the collective sense of being tyrannized by time, and this sharing may also serve to offset the feeling of aloneness in the face of such tyranny. It's not uncommon to hear a coworker or family member bemoan how time is flying by or the days seem to blur together. In this one-line poem, George Swede succinctly combines life's transience and the sound of the clock:

falling pine needles   the tick of the clock

Margaret Chula, reflecting a Buddhist view, roots herself in the here-and-now:

> this moment
> is all—cracks
> in the stone Buddha

Denis M. Garrison realizes that the convergence between death and the ending of time culminates in stillness, where the separation between self and world is transcended:

> and when
> the sand runs out?
> the stillness
> of the hourglass
> and I are one

Emptiness

A number of poets grappled with the implications of our transient nature. If there is nothing permanent about human existence, if there is nothing to grasp or hold onto, then life itself appears inherently empty. It takes great courage to behold emptiness, which usually fills people with terror, yet doing so is anything but nihilistic.

Scott Galasso writes with great sensitivity and compassion:

island in the mist—
the empty snail shell
casts no shadow

And S. B. Friedman, invoking the ancient Chinese philosophy of Taoism (also spelled Daoism), suggests that emptiness (like death) is no less a part of life than all we embrace during our lifetime:

the dao gathers in emptiness winter chill

Impermanence

To make peace with the chill of emptiness is to free ourselves from attachment (clinging or craving in Buddhism). So much of life is about seeking to fulfill our desires, longings, aspirations. Yet, insofar as life is intrinsically ephemeral, there is nothing we really can hold onto, in the final analysis. As meditation teacher Stephen Levine has observed: If we don't get the teaching that everything is impermanent during our lifetime, we get a crash course at the end.

Letting go of our attachments is what Scott Galasso and Thom Williams are nudging us toward in these poems:

letting go
this life,
autumn leaves

End of summer
Just another thing
I can't hang on to

Invoking the everyday image of a common weed, Stanford M. Forrester eloquently conveys the essence of transience:

that's what
dandelions do . . .
blow away

God and Faith

Interestingly, only a few poets alluded to God or heaven while contemplating their own mortality. Robin Beshers depicts a domestic scene, attending to an apple tree in her backyard:

Wondering about God
I pluck flawed apples
from the tree

Marilyn F. Johnston is tentative about her faith in God but is prepared to believe:

if there's a god
in Adieu!
that's the god I believe in

Ernest Berry can't wait to get home from the doctor's office where the results from a recent biopsy have thrust death in his face, abruptly and unexpectedly. To manage his anxiety, if not panic, he hops on the computer and does an internet search:

biopsy
i google
god

We don't know what the poet found in cyberspace; as for the reader. . .

With tongue in cheek, Ruth Holzer presents a pedestrian poem about death as part of the local bus route:

boarding
the number eighteen bus
to heaven

David Lanoue, on the other hand, is content to remain on this plane—
the plane of Nature:

no heaven, no hell
just the whispering
rushes

Details

A good many poets grapple with the practical aspects of death; that is,
funeral arrangements, the manner in which one's body will be disposed
of; details regarding one's gravestone.

Wisteria scent —
where I'd have my ashes
scattered

   —John Brandi

it doesn't matter
where the beach is, or how
you get me there . . .
lay me on a sheet of wind
like a sand mandala

   —Michael McClintock

write me a haiku
in two languages
for my grave stone

   —Margaret Chula

Raymond Roseliep, a Catholic priest and poet, slides back the veil which

25

separates himself (and the reader) from a tactile encounter with death:

ordering my tombstone:
the cutter has me feel
the Gothic "R"

Of course, there is the secret wish, the wordless longing, to be spared from death, after all. One hopes and prays for a last minute stay of execution. Cherie Hunter Day gives voice to the universal plea one makes to the so-called Grim Reaper, to God, to no one in particular, to be passed over:

crimson maple
maybe death
won't recognize me

When does the reality of death first come into awareness? Surprisingly, only one poet traced back the birth of death awareness to a moment in childhood:

Seven or eight
first shudder at my own death
walking home from school

—Bruce England

Naturally, one's own mortality affects others. Nothing is more poignant for a parent than when his or her child suddenly realizes that mommy or daddy is going to die one day. The precocious among us, like Bruce England in the previous poem, glimpse the reality of death some forty or fifty years (if we're lucky) before it happens:

And so I agree
not to die before she does
the sound of crickets

—Susan Antolin

Matter-of-factly
my daughter asks,
"What day will you die?"

—Bruce England

It takes great courage to admit one's fear of death to oneself, let alone to others. While some may turn to prayer or to Nature for comfort and consolation, Michael Ketchek exposes the nakedness of dread, using sharp irony to capture an all-too-human truth:

thinking about death
I reach for a cigarette
to calm down

Afterlife

Ideas like reincarnation and heaven may have originated in our attempt to allay death anxiety. Regarding life after death, two poets represent the continuum between which the rest of us fall:

one bead at a time
counting
on an afterlife

—Susan La Vallee

flagstone patio
never believed in an afterlife
still don't

—Michael Ketchek

But john martone faces his future here-and-now, knowing what we are made of:

rubbing earth
    on my face
        my future face

Humor

Humor appears indispensable in facing the hardships and adversities we face in life. Then why not with death, too? With humor we find a way to bear the unbearable, to take the inevitable not-so-seriously, as in Andrew Shattuck McBride's poem:

plotting
my green
burial

Or Jim Milstead's:

Only dead silence
Where is the heavenly choir
are angels on strike?

Humor does not deny the insults and injuries we endure on the long and winding road; it sheds light when we find ourselves in a dark wood. Humor is our flashlight, a candle, a match, that enables us to see just enough to take the next—or last—step. I dare say that most of us wouldn't have gotten as far as we have without a touch of light-heartedness. "Like the man who went to the psychiatrist and said, 'I'm afraid I'm going to die.' And the psychiatrist reassured him, 'That's the last thing you're going to do.'" (1) For another example of humor around one's own mortality, see vincent tripi's poem below.

Homecoming

For many death is the ultimate journey home. Take these two haiku by Robert Spiess and Carlos Colon, respectively:

the field's evening fog—
quietly the hound comes
to fetch me home

pointing
my way home
the starfish (2)

These poems are about homecoming and hold special meaning for me, as my parents uprooted me at the tender age of thirteen when my father obtained a new job in another state. My sense of home was shattered; it wasn't until I rediscovered love years later that I reclaimed my sense of home.

Often in life we feel cast out of our homes and it seems to us as though we must embark on a journey to return. The metaphor of journey pervades the poetry of both East and West. Roberta Beary punctuates her journey with fireflies—a familiar and poignant symbol of impermanence.

It lights up
as lightly as it fades:
a firefly

Birth itself may seem like the primal expulsion, turning life into a long journey home, the latter being sometimes equated with death, a return to Mother Earth, from which we all originate. This reunion is what Edith Shiffert intimates in her serene haiku:

Before the great change
lie at ease upon the earth—
soon you will have it.

Or. . . The earth will have us.

Ruth Franke, in her essay on American death poems, goes so far as to assert that American haiku poets are fascinated with death because, consciously or unconsciously, we seek death. She invokes Sigmund Freud, who postulated what he called the "death drive"—an unconscious wish to die, as though doing so was equated with a return to the womb. Deriving a death drive from the reality of death is a bit like deducing that, because hunger is a drive, there is a concomitant "evacuation wish or instinct." Most contemporary psychoanalysts—at least in America—have debunked Freud's belief in a death instinct (3), but it persists in the minds of some, nonetheless. Once again, I suggest that birth and death may, in the last analysis, be likened to starfish pointing toward that which lies beyond the field of knowledge and experience, residing in the ineffable.

Mystery

Without a permanent self or world to hold onto, what's left? It is very evident to me that life is, as I have already suggested, fundamentally and ineradicably a mystery. "Death," Emily Dickinson declared, "is a wild night and a new road." Far from evoking terror or despair, I delight in, if not celebrate this realization, as do many other poets in this collection.

John Stevenson is one of them. He does not appear to be put off by the mystery that is life-and-death. On the contrary, the mystery is all together evocative in an almost Whitmanesque way, as in this subtle haiku:

seated between us
the imaginary
middle passenger

Last Writes

To fully embrace the mystery that is life-and-death, what can one say, in the last analysis? In facing death head-on, everything is washed away: All beliefs, ideas, illusions, theories, even images.

What remains for those who have the courage to gaze down the well is poetry stripped bare, reflecting what in Buddhist meditation is known as "bare attention." Toko, a Japanese poet who died in 1795 at the age of eighty-six, encapsulated bare attention by exposing the very writing of death poems as a form of clinging or attachment:

death poems
are mere delusion—
death is death

Of course, there is a mystifying irony in Toko's death poem, quoted in
JAPANESE DEATH POEMS, because it contains an existential truth
even as it preserves the very form it decries. Perhaps the best death
poems hint at a riddle or conundrum that leaves the reader bedeviled or
bemused insofar as the answer or solution to death eludes the rational
mind.

In the following death poem written by contemporary poet Karma
Tenzing Wanghuk, it is unclear whether the poet is echoing or
responding to Toko's death poem:

no
death
poem

Is Tenzing suggesting (a la Buddhism) that there is no death and, hence,
no death poem; or that no death poem can be written by anyone who is
still alive and kicking?

Undeterred by such metaphysical questions, vincent tripi mischievously
invokes Bashō's most famous frog haiku (4):

> The old pond
>   my death poem
>   plop!

tripi's poem is about as far from morbid as one can get. He links past
and present by harking back to the ancient pond that the father of haiku
brilliantly depicted in his original poem, which was not his last poem. In
substituting his own death poem for the frog of Bashō's haiku, tripi is
playfully suggesting that our death, like our life, contains amphibian-like
qualities; our death, like us, can adapt to changing circumstances, forms,
or media. As for that inimitable sound the frog makes when jumping in
. . . Well, there is perhaps no more perfect sound for a death poem, after

all is said and done, than plop.

Ah, That

I recognize that "plop" may not satisfy one and all as the last word (or sound) on the mystery that is life-and-death. What, then, could this unfathomable question mark at the center of our lives be pointing us toward? One possible answer, I think, could lie in what the author of WALDEN realized while mourning the untimely death of his older brother, John, of lockjaw. "The only remedy for love," he confided in his journal, "is to love more."

We certainly know what happens where love is absent: People grow old and bitter; their hearts close, they become depressed, demoralized, despairing. Their days are filled with complaints, regrets, and an impatient longing to die in hopes of escaping the prison of this so-called vale of tears.

Among the poets included here, there is little trace of bitterness, resentment, regret. I dare say that love abounds, however subtly, in many of the poems. In fact, it is really the medium of love that enables fear, anger, disappointment, loneliness, and sadness to float, as mindfulness meditation teacher, Stephen Levine, is fond of saying.

Thirty-five years ago, our family dog, whose name was Corky, was whisked away by our father, when we were all out of the house on a winter Sunday. Dad was well-meaning in his desire to spare us the anguish of taking Corky to the vet to put him down. A month or so before Corky died at the age of seventeen, I had a short dream about him that remains with me still: He and I were jogging to the freeway entrance near my parents' house. Just as we were about to enter the freeway, Corky veered off to the right and, as he jumped effortlessly over a chain link fence that ran along the freeway, he turned to me and said, "We must continue on, lovingly."

Though I had this dream long before I trained as a psychologist, it was one that required no interpretation; the meaning and significance of the dream were instantly clear to me, and I have drawn strength and courage from Corky's message during many losses in the intervening years.

Love, then, becomes all the more vital in living with the unfathomable, with loneliness, illness, pain, uncertainty, and the ultimate loss of everything dear to us. Thoreau, a Transcendentalist, understood this sacred truth, which is why he had no trouble declaring his faith in a letter to a contemporary: "Our religion is where our love is."

Yet, love is not a quality of consciousness that can be cultivated or called forth by an act of will. Love is a well, an indwelling, accessible whenever one's heart is open. I open my heart when I am encouraged, and when I am encouraged, I am more inclined to act courageously. It is no accident that these words are related. Their Latin root is cor, which means heart.

Haiku, I suggest, is a poetry of the heart; it is a repository of love. To write haiku is to realize from moment to moment that the world is whole and we are an integral part of that whole. As a sometime student of Zen, Bashō, the father of Japanese haiku, apprehended the truth of wholeness centered in the here-and-now (5). Virtually all of his haiku are written from this place, which is why, I suspect, he responded to a request from his students for a death poem, by saying that any of his poems could be considered his death poem. They persisted and he relented, writing the poem that inspired the title of this anthology, a few days before he died:

Sick, on a journey,
Yet over withered fields
Dreams wander on. (5)

Dreams wander on, and we ourselves must find a way to continue on, lovingly. . . until we breathe our last. This, I suggest, is what links the ancient Japanese poets with the contemporary haiku poets writing in the West. (6) We have taken Bashō's advice to heart and sought what the ancients sought, rather than merely echo their poetic spirit. What we have found is already merging with the wind in the pines.

NOTES

1. Quoted in Steven Harrison, THE LOVE OF UNCERTAINTY. pp. 35-36.

2. In her essay, "American Death Poems," Ruth Franke regards the starfish in Colon's haiku as reflecting uncertainty as to which way leads home. An alternative interpretation (among many) is possible: To the extent that the reality of death is accepted as an inextricable part of life, one may return home by heading in any direction.

3. See, for example, A. J. Levin. The Fiction of the Death Instinct. Psychoanalytic Quarterly, 21, 275-276, 1951 and Otto Fenichel, THE PSYCHOANALYTIC THEORY OF NEUROSIS. NY: W. W. Norton, 1945. Of Freud's death drive, Swiss psychiatrist Carl Jung had little more than passing interest in, as he put it, the "questionable nature of the conception." TWO ESSAYS ON ANALYTICAL PSYCHOLOGY. Princeton, NJ: Princeton University Press, 1966. p. 29.

4. Bashō's frog haiku: old pond/a frog jumps in/plop! (Alan Watts, translator)

5. Bashō Death Poem from: ZEN POEMS OF CHINA AND JAPAN: THE CRANE'S BILL. Copyright 1973 Stryk, L., Ikemoto, T., and Takayama, T., translators. New York, NY: Grove Press, 1994. Used by permission of Grove/Atlantic, Inc.

6. Out of respect for those who have worked sedulously to divorce haiku from Zen, I want to emphasize that one need not be a follower of Zen or a student of Buddhism to write haiku or death awareness poems. Still, there is an attunement in Zen to matters of life-and-death with which I deeply resonate; hence, the references to Zen that appear throughout the Introduction and for which I take full responsibility.

Robert Epstein
El Cerrito, California
6 October 2010

Dreams Wander On

I'll return to earth
graceful as spent Irises
bid farewell to June

—Carlene Adams

winter day
    wildflower rosettes
on the plot reserved for me

—Linda Ahrens

wondering
    who else
visits my headstone

—Linda Ahrens

Talking again
about life and death
under the spring moon

—Eric Amann, *Cicada Voices*, 1983

Robert Epstein

when my whole note
and the universe are ready
there will be a tap
on my shoulder—and my song
shall fly beyond me

—Kay Anderson, *Red Lights*, 2:2, 2006

the cemetery gate swung open i go first

—frances angela, *moonset*, 4. 2, 2008

and so I agree
not to die before she does
the sound of crickets

—Susan Antolin, *Artichoke Season*, 2009

birth–death

this stretch of beach
between

an'ya

an'ya, *DailyHaiga.org*, 2009

simmering tofu—
father asks me where I intend
to be buried

   —Fay Aoyagi, *Acorn,* #24, 2010

first snow
my spirit pauses
before dropping my body

   —Belia Archuleta

Rain clouds overhead
a deep, black silence—a flash
we live and are gone

   —Jim Bainbridge

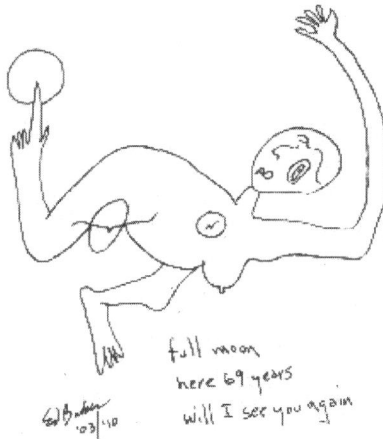

full moon
here 69 years
will I see you again

Ed Baker, *Modern Haiku, 39.1,* 2008; slightly revised from original

Robert Epstein

clouds low on the hills
I grow old in the lingering chill
and the rain is steady

  —Jerry Ball

last goodbye
turning cold
sumac leaves

  —Francine Banwarth, *Modern Haiku, 41.1*, 2010

in the prison graveyard
just as he was in life—
convict 14302

  --Johnny Baranski, *just a stone's throw*, 2006

into the silence
the grasshopper sings
into the night

  —John Barlow, *Notes from the Gean, 2:2*, 2010

eddy
after eddy, after eddy . . .
autumn river,
can you possibly share my longing
for the great unknown?

—John Barlow, *Tangled Hair, 3*, 2001

lone hiker
the trail ends where sky
and desert meet

—Edith Bartholomeusz, *Hummingbird, XIX: 1*, 2008

on my finger
the firefly puts out
its light

—Roberta Beary, *The Unworn Necklace*, 2007

biopsy
i google
god

—Ernest Berry

Robert Epstein

mri
my death haiku
revised

—Ernest Berry

death haiku —
but what if I die
sudd

—Ernest Berry

wondering about God
I pluck flawed apples
from the tree

—Robin Beshers

Not quite dark   silent
listening with near still breath
welcoming the wolf

—Philip Boatright, *Sparrows*, 2008

swept up whirling
leaves, shreds, dust and down
their shadows circling

—Dan Brady

Wisteria scent—
where I'd have my ashes
scattered

    —John Brandi

Old age—
he begins to notice
every cremation tower

    —John Brandi

Whitewater—
the swiftness of life
banked with sorrow

    —John Brandi

his last poem
all ready
in the drawer

    —John Brandi

Now that fallen leaves
have buried the path
the trail is clear

    —John Brandi, *The Unswept Path*, 2005

43   *Robert Epstein*

visiting my brother's grave
I see the plot
reserved for me

 —Bob Brill

the wind slaps my face
with a sheet of newspaper
obituary

 —Bob Brill

lunch in the courtyard—
cherry blossom obscuring
the hands of the clock

 —Helen Buckingham, Runner-up, 57th Bashō Festival Association
Award, 2003

night's end a muffled chirrup

 —Helen Buckingham, *Wisteria, #11*, 2008

fossil
older
by the second

 —Helen Buckingham, *3 Lights Gallery*, 2008

journey's end
a sudden gust
lavender fields

—Helen Buckingham, Runner-up, Bashō's 360th Anniversary Web
Haiku Contest, 2003

all soul's day . . .
the last hold of leaves
on the tree

—Marjorie A. Buettner

watching
the clock's hand shift
from here to there
where is this place
called infinity

—Marjorie A. Buettner

dark of the moon . . .
closer to the mysteries
that surround

—Marjorie A. Buettner

Robert Epstein

today I am
one of the waning leaves
on the courgette plant

 —Owen Bullock

dried leaves . . .
am I delaying
the inevitable?

 —Owen Bullock

when dead
will I be some
particle
floating
through space?

 —Owen Bullock

after my death
a hermit thrush
sings

 —Allan Burns

into the mists
i too
become one

    —Tom Camp

before the firing squad
        the perfect ash
of a last cigar

    —David Caruso, *Roadrunner, IX:2,* 2009

i believe i'll float a while
before i settle . . . dust

    —David Caruso, *bottle rockets, #21,* 2009

miriam chaikin   has left   this world

    —miriam chaikin

mausoleum—
just passing
through

    —Yu Chang, *The Heron's Nest, 8,* 2006

        Robert Epstein

bearing down
on a borrowed pen
do not resuscitate

—Yu Chang, *The Heron's Nest, 11*, 2009

cemetery gate
she lets me
go first

—Yu Chang, *Upstate Dim Sum*, 2009

this moment
is all—cracks
in the stone Buddha

—Margaret Chula, *The Smell of Rust*, 2003

write me a haiku
in two languages
for my grave stone

—Margaret Chula, *Grinding My Ink*, 1993

this life
from darkness
into darkness
with only a few fireflies
to light our way

    —Margaret Chula, *Always Filling, Always Full*, 2001

walking the path
through the dark garden
 moonlight shines
    on the flower
        with no scent

    —Margaret Chula, *Ribbons, 5:2*, 2009, Members Choice Tanka

LISTENING

by the window,
leaves ripple —
waves
being pulled ashore
at low tide.

    —Dave Church, *bear creek haiku, #85*, 2008

Robert Epstein

for all that
which I will not get to
do in this life
the fountain carries on
in the rain

    —Tom Clausen, *bottle rockets, #13*, 2005

dew-heavy grass
each footstep on the lawn
marks something done

    --David Cobb, *Spitting Pips*, 2009

all the poems
I've written
melting snow

    —Carlos Colon, *Frogpond, 33:1*, 2010

lung condition
my one-breath poems
grow shorter

    —Carlos Colon, *Modern Haiku, 41.1*, 2010

pointing
my way home
the starfish

    —Carlos Colon, *Raw NerVZ, 3:1*, 1996

endless horizon —
the stars reflected
in my pool

    —Steven E. Cottingham

ebb tide
the shell I keep reaching for
carried further away

    —John Crook, *Ebb Tide: Selected Haiku*, 2003

a chill at sunset
the empty snail shell
casts no shadow

    —William Cullen, Jr., *Notes from the Gean, 1:4*, 2010

island in the mist
a lone figure waits
on the ferry pier

    —William Cullen, Jr., *Acorn, #20*, 2008

Robert Epstein

last call
my empty glass
full of moonlight

    —William Cullen, Jr.

heaven's stream
the tide takes back
my footprints

    —William Cullen, Jr.

An early departure
The painful tug of ten o'clock
I am not ready.

    —Anne Curran

a lone raindrop —
the short journey from
cloud to ocean

    —Norman Darlington, *Haiku Sansaar*, 2008

relinquishing the menu
today I eat the mountains
drink the sky

    —Norman Darlington

beyond
stars beyond
star

   —L. A. Davidson, *The Shape of the Tree*, 1982

crimson maples
maybe death
won't recognize me

   —Cherie Hunter Day, *Frogpond 28*: 3, 2005

a brown moth
folded on the windowsill
an expiration date
on my cereal box—
as if I needed reminders

   --Cherie Hunter Day, *American Tanka, 17*, 2008

calcified coil
as it tumbles in the surf
my mind considers
death as a full halt
with more motion afterwards

   —Cherie Hunter Day, *e-LYNX, XVI:3*, 2001

the downward rush
of black-shouldered kites
on a hillside tangle
   death will come out of nowhere
   with just such accuracy

   —Cherie Hunter Day, *Tangled Hair, 4*, 2004

once so lovely
but now the withered lilies
are pale reminders
how easily
they come apart in my hands

   Cherie Hunter Day, *Kindle of Green*, 2008

crystals
      of
snow
     . . . gone. . .
  rain-
    fall

   —Raffael de Gruttola

all the difference
between life and death
a simple straw

—Raffael de Gruttola

This is the approach that Japanese monks would use when they knew death was imminent i.e. burying themselves in the earth. Their last moments were to breathe through a straw that was extended from their burial crypt or mound to the air above. —Poet's note

in the sea
I have
a cool coffin

—Raffael de Gruttola

in darkness
the smell of the candle
blown out

—Bruce Detrick, *Five O' Clock Shadow*, 2000

the trail so long
my flashlight
dimming

—Charles B. Dickson

Robert Epstein

spring wind—
I too
am dust

    —Patricia Donegan, *The Unswept Path*, 2005

sunrise . . .
half a clam shell
nudged by a wave

    —Connie Donleycott

making way
for others—
autumn trail

    —George Dorsty

a last letter—
only the the stamp
is forever

    —George Dorsty

hospice window—
a house finch
looks in on me

    —George Dorsty

death bed—
my change
on the dresser

—George Dorsty

a red maple leaf
settles among the others—
my last breath

—Wende Skidmore DuFlon

our last deal—
I'll wait for you
on the Elysian Fields

—Wendy Skidmore Duflon

dead man's curve—
a screech owl veers
toward the river

—Curtis Dunlap, *The Heron's Nest, 11*, 2009

the first autumn
I plant
no spring-flowering bulbs

—John J. Dunphy

Robert Epstein

cemetery
I touch my newly-purchased lot
with one foot

—John J. Dunphy

Seven or eight
first shudder at my own death
walking home from school

—Bruce England

Matter-of-factly
my daughter asks,
"what day will you die?"

—Bruce England

Those at my bed
will see that a darkness
came over my eyes

—Bruce England

when it's time to go
open the window and I'll follow
the songbird home

—Robert Epstein

checkout time is noon
I turn in the key
and everything else

 —Robert Epstein

in pine shade
I forget a while
this life will end

 —Robert Epstein, *moonset, 6:1*, 2010

that way home
falling
cherry blossoms

 —Robert Epstein, *bottle rockets, #24*, 2011

deathbed window
moonlight through
trembling aspens

 —Robert Epstein

rummage sale —
selling the moment of my life
to pay for what's left

 —Seren Fargo

childless
my memories passed
only to paper

—Seren Fargo

death poem —
refusing to complete
this last . . .

—Seren Fargo

center stage
dreading
the last applause

—Seren Fargo

having already
left my heart behind
I finally leave the rest

—Seren Fargo

cherry blossoms falling
cherry blossoms falling
someday I won't exist

—Michael Fessler, *bottle rockets, #22,* 2010

to be in decline
while everything is growing
always contrary

   —Michael Fessler

Shelf of Best Sellers . . .
What will be the last book I read —
The last sentence?

   —Michael Fessler, *bottle rockets, #22,* 2010

the snow
newly fallen —one day
i will not be here

   —Donna Fleischer, *Ko,* 2005

even as
I turn away . . .
sun casts
my shadow

   —Donna Fleischer

Ten times ten thousand
   terrible things in this world
     and still I don't want to leave it

   —Sylvia Forges-Ryan

Robert Epstein

Let me die
        the night after
                the first daylily blooms

    —Sylvia Forges-Ryan

After I'm gone
        where will you find me
                if not in my poems

    —Sylvia Forges-Ryan

taking
everything back . . .
ebb tide

    — Stanford M. Forrester

death poem—
    what happens
            if I don't write one

    —Stanford M. Forrester

reincarnation—
already have a death poem
from the last time

    —Stanford M. Forrester

writing a haiku
in the sand . . .
a wave finishes it

   —Stanford M. Forrester, *Chiyo's Corner, 3.1*, 2001

that's what
dandelions do . . .
blow away

   —Stanford M. Forrester, *Poetalk*, 2001

outgoing tide
a boat comes loose
from its anchor

   —Alice Frampton

autumn leaves
floating
in a soft breeze—
how hard
to be so light

   —Ruth Franke, *Slipping through Water*, 2010.

returning to the Way—
no blame.
  jasmine fragrance.

  —S. B. Friedman

the dao gathers in emptiness winter chill

  —S. B. Friedman

rain turns to snow silence

  —S. B. Friedman

to die a little bit each day: bird beak w
                                          o
                                            r
                                              m

  —S. B. Friedman, *Modern Haiku, 39:2,* 2008

a bag of bones writing poetry for what?

  —S. B. Friedman

how many breaths left?
  buttercup shoots
    poke through the snow

  —S. B. Friedman

letting go
this life,
autumn leaves

  —Scott Galasso, *Laughing Out Clouds*, 2007

I wasn't
then I was
now I'm not

  —Scott Galasso, *Sea, Mist and Sitka Spruce*, 2010

one breath
the difference between
I am and I was

  —Scott Galasso, *moonset, 4. 2*, 2008

the longest night—
the death poem
rustles

  —D. Claire Gallagher, *The Heron's Nest*, 9, 2007

Robert Epstein

our family plot
a place for everyone
but me

—Brenda Gannam

draped all in black
and carrying a scythe—
my date for Halloween

—Brenda Gannam

after the funeral
slipping my bare feet
into Dad's old shoes

—Brenda Gannam

every day this wind
one day when it comes
my breath will leave with it

—Denis M. Garrison, *Twitter*, 2009

flying to the light
I glimpse the earth one last time—
vast red peony

—Denis M. Garrison, *FlyingFishes.net*, 2006

poems
written in dust
a windy day

—Denis M. Garrison, *Hidden River*, 2006

the flies . . .
the flies . . .
will no one close my eyes?

—Denis M. Garrison, *FlyingFishes.net*, 2006

and when
the sand runs out?
the stillness
of the hourglass
and I are one

—Denis M. Garrison, *Modern English Tanka, 5*, 2007

Robert Epstein

River stones
worn smooth
I have no regrets

   —Garry Gay

Farewell—
to the geese
and the autumn moon

   —Garry Gay

To see Void vast infinite
look out the window
into the blue sky.

   —Allen Ginsberg, *Death and Fame: Last Poems*, 2000

borrowed time . . .
leaving a nickel
in the change slot

—Peter Joseph Gloviczki, *Modern Haiku, 40.2,* 2009

lull me, muse,
into the wavering belief
that my tanka
will walk me
to the end of the road

—Sanford Goldstein, *Tanka Journal, 20,* 2002

at the final site
listening to the stark poems
of others,
he wonders if some word-maker
will offer him a thirty-one

—Sanford Goldstein, *Four Decades on My Tanka Road,* 2007

Robert Epstein

a drop of blood
on the sheet

a few words
on the water

   —Michael Gregory

in that calm
accepting

plenitude

quickening
the air

   —Michael Gregory

clinging to the rock
through gales of laughter.

   —Michael Gregory

the final journey
requires traveling light—
signs read "no baggage"

   —Maxine Grodjinksy

skeleton key
to the box of photos—
last possession

—Maxine Grodjinksy

frozen branches
measure the emptiness—
winter sunset

—Lee Gurga, *The Measure of Emptiness*, 1991

plum blossoms
I make plans
for my ashes

—Carolyn Hall, *Modern Haiku, 37.2*, 2006, First Prize, Robert Spiess
Memorial Award

at last I shall roam
the rice fields where my ancestors
left their footprints

—John J. Han

towards dusk
all the pain from the past
makes my steps lighter

—John J. Han

time to depart—
erasing memories
gazing at the lotus

    —John J. Han

a time of stillness
and for peaceful reflection
before the tide turns

    —Dan Hardison

scatter my dust
under trees that buck
in the summer rain

    —William Hart, *bear creek haiku, #99*, 2008

broken bowl
the pieces
still rocking

    —Penny Harter, *In the Broken Curve*, 1984

another birthday
I push the candles in
deeper

    —Penny Harter, *Brocade of Leaves*, 2003

harder than dying
is being reborn
spring buds

 —Peggy Heinrich

fallen petals
how special each day
of the rose

 —Peggy Heinrich

froth spits at wind
how far must I travel
to find placid water?

 —Peggy Heinrich

lost at last,
among old growth cedars
sound of the river

 —Christopher Herold

   Robert Epstein

river's end
the sound of my name in the hiss
of receding surf

 —Christopher Herold

death dream . . .
I struggle awake to the cry
of a mourning dove

 —William J. Higginson, *The Unswept Path*, 2005

smell of bile . . .
I wake to October
afterglow

 —William J. Higginson, *Frogpond, 32: 1*, 2009

October afterglow
will my lucky star
shine tonight?

 —William J. Higginson, *Frogpond, 32: 1*, 2009

hospital window
in the clear dawn sky
one full moon

 —William J. Higginson, *Frogpond, 32:1*, 2009

The clock
　　chimes, chimes and stops,
　　　　but the river . . .

　　—William J. Higginson, HSA haiku contest winner, 1969

winter sun
my face reflected
in the polished headstone

　　—Paul Hodder, *Paper Wasp*, 2006

driving to Jersey
reciting
Japanese death poems

　　—Ruth Holzer, *bottle rockets, #9*, 2003

boarding
the number eighteen bus
to heaven

　　—Ruth Holzer

not everything
has a solution—
autumn leaves

　　—Ruth Holzer, *Silk Flower*, 2005

in the dead of night—
my thoughts turned
to my next breath

    —Gary Hotham, *Quadrant, #396*, 2003

footprints left
in the morning snow—
still mine

    —Gary Hotham, *Wisteria*, 2006

    fading daylight—
the sounds as the ocean
        runs out

    —Gary Hotham, *bottle rockets, #21*, 2009

driving in through the Funeral Home's EXIT ONLY

    —Marshall Hryciuk, *Modern Haiku, 36.2*, 2005

the dark cloud
slowly lifts
and I see
snow covered hills
shining in distant sunlight

    —Gerry Jacobson, *Tea Towel Tanka*, 2008

If there's a god
in Adieu!
that's the god I believe in

 —Marilyn E. Johnston, *bottle rockets, #15*, 2006

summit photo and the sky only a few feet away

 —Jim Kacian

mile high . . .
my breath mingles
with the clouds

 —Jim Kacian, *The Heron's Nest, 11*, 2009

short poems prepared to meet my unmaker

 —Jim Kacian

fogged in and my own light shining back

 —Jim Kacian

Robert Epstein

walking slowly
on autumn's oak leaves
I select one
brittle and brown
as the hand that lets it go

— Kirsty Karkow

release them now
the lines that tether
my little boat
I am lured by the light
on that faraway island

—Kirsty Karkow

homeward bound—
pushing my paddle
through the wind

—Kirsty Karkow, *Magnapoets, 3*, 2009

sliding, sliding
off the icy road . . .
now what?

—Kirsty Karkow

this strong desire
to go the unmarked way
a scrap of sun
highlights the snowy path
starting at my feet

—Kirsty Karkow

grains of sand drift
over bleached bones
of those who came before—
how much more warning
do you need?

—Michael Ketchek, *Modern English Tanka*, 2008

ancient fossil
rests on my palm
the shallow crease of my life line

—Michael Ketchek, *Frogpond, 33:1*, 2010

thinking about death
I reach for a cigarette
to calm down

—Michael Ketchek, *Hermitage*, 2005

Robert Epstein

flagstone patio
never believed in an afterlife
still don't

    —Michael Ketchek, *Raw NerVZ, 4:4*, 1998

after I am gone
break my plate
bury my pen
plant flowers
in my cup

    —Michael Ketchek, *Ribbons, 2:4*, 2007

terminally ill . . .
the unopened buds
on an orchid stem

    —Jerry Kilbride, *bottle rockets, #14*, 2006

deathbed
the pesky fly
mightier than I

    —Jerry Kilbride, *bottle rockets, #14*, 2006

terminally ill . . .
when I was a kid I tried
to count all the stars

 —Jerry Kilbride, *bottle rockets, #14* 2006

last breath
finally it's over
now I can relax

 —Howard Lee Kilby

last breath
remembering her kisses
is plenty

 —Howard Lee Kilby

with my last breath
I'm sure I will say
I wish I had lived in Japan

 —Howard Lee Kilby

the apple blossoms
early this year . . .
time to update my will

 —John Kinory, *Modern Haiku, 40.3,* 2009

          Robert Epstein

the autumn moon
suddenly moves off
my vanished shadow

—Joseph Kirschner

at the end
of a long path
goldenrod both sides

—Karen Klein, *Wind Flow*, 2008

moans, groans and trombones
from the couch to the coffin
old bones

—Susan Marie La Vallee

sunset—
the shadow of Diamond Head
long and dark as a death

—Susan Marie La Vallee

dead of winter—
the man in the moon
disappears

—Susan Marie La Vallee

one bead at a time
counting
on an afterlife

—Susan Marie La Vallee, *Frogpond, 32:1*, 2009

when that day comes
will there be one moment
for my own death haiku?

—Elizabeth Searle Lamb

still wanting
to fly   these feathers
of the dead owl

—Elizabeth Searle Lamb, *The Heron's Nest, 4*, 2004

no heaven, no hell
just the whispering
rushes

—David G. Lanoue

ice-skimmed pond
the cries of wild geese
            fainter and fainter

—Catherine J. S. Lee

Robert Epstein

white moths
flicker into darkness . . .
a thousand stars

—Catherine J. S. Lee

low clouds or high fog
heaven glimpsed through black pines
peace now and later

—Michael Henry Lee

after the viewing
this major body of work
esteemed at last

—Michael Henry Lee

four AM oldies
sounding in every joint
like that old swan song

—Michael Henry Lee

Autumn evening—
yellow leaves cover
the plot reserved for me

—Rebecca Lilly, *Shadwell Hills*, 2002

death

   at last I won't be bothered
   by flies

      —Bob Lucky

a gust of wind
my kite runs out
of string

      —Bob Lucky

not quite goodbye—
an ocean breaks
against rocks

      —Peggy Willis Lyles, *Modern Haiku, 40.3*, 2009

into the afterlife red leaves

   Peggy Willis Lyles, *Modern Haiku, 41.1*, 2010

yes, this too
could be my life—
a few stones
mixed with bright bits of glass
left scattered on a grave

      —Carole MacRury, *Modern English Tanka 2:1*, 2007

Robert Epstein

this life
so like a mushroom
rising up
to greet the dawn
and dying back at dusk

—Carole MacRury

an empty shell
fills with moonlight—
winter's end

—Carole MacRury and Ion Crudescu, *In the Company of Crows: Haiku and Tanka Between the Tides*, 2008

find me in the sounds
of sparkling brooks . . . young leaves
songs of forest birds

 —Robert Mainone, *Modern Haiku, 41.2*, 2010

a passing moment
in the great mystery
of whirling stars

 —Robert Mainone

nightfall

i'm
glowing

gold
on

the
road

between
obscure

and
obsolete

 —Ed Markowski

deathpoemthelightbetweentheletters

—Ed Markowski, *bottle rockets, #21*, 2009

death bed
    the shadow of a peach tree
on three feet of snow

    —Ed Markowski

you're part of this secret

    —john martone, *tumulus*, 2006

alone
    all you've
        brought with you

    —john martone, *tumulus*, 2006

my
second-
hand

drawer
some

day
second-

hand
again

    —john martone, *stem*, 2004

rubbing earth
   on my face
      my future face

    — john martone, *tumulus*, 2006

a whitetail flickers
   into birch . . .
what time I have left

    —Scott Mason, First Place, 2006 Betty Drevniok Competition

        Robert Epstein

my death poem
   rejected
I carry on

   —Scott Mason

august rain knowing I must depart

   —Scott Mason, *Modern Haiku, 40.3*, 2009

bucket of mums   covered with bees   . . . days grow short

   —Diane Mayr, *Run, Turkey, Run!*, 2007

with samaras twirling
to earth, I shuffle to
my last appointment

   —Andrew Shattuck McBride

nights taking statins
contemplating
my end

   —Andrew Shattuck McBride

plotting
my green
burial

   —Andrew Shattuck McBride

it doesn't matter
where the beach is, or how
you get me there . . .
lay me on a sheet of wind,
like a sand mandala

   —Michael McClintock, *Gusts*, 2005

when life ends
the number of things
I leave undone
will be fewer, if today
I tell no lies

   —Michael McClintock, *Modern English Tanka, 1:1*, 2006

so this is death—
bidding friends goodnight,
the last cookie eaten

   —Michael McClintock, *Modern Haiku, 37.1*, 2006

Robert Epstein

death poem—
the no sound
of snowflakes

    —Tyrone McDonald, *Modern Haiku, 39.2,* 2008

test results
my breath poem flits away
on a breath of air

    —Fonda Bell Miller

stinging nettle
my death poem's
elusive punch line

    —Fonda Bell Miller

scattered leaves
what I will
leave behind

    —paul m., *Modern Haiku, 36.2,* 2005

saw-toothed peaks-
leave my body
to wild dogs

    —paul m. *Called Home,* 2005

migrating whales
all our footprints
wash away

 —paul m., *The Heron's Nest, 4*, 2002

diseased hemlock
its shade
my shade

 —paul m., *Lilliput Review*, in press

summer's end
riding a borrowed bicycle
past the graveyard

 —paul m., *Finding the Way: Haiku and Field Notes*, 2002

Cul-de-sac ahead
Warning: one entrance, no exit
Enter at your own risk

 —Jim Milstead

Only dead silence
Where is the heavenly choir
are angels on strike?

 —Jim Milstead

Robert Epstein

Winter tragedy:
Famous comedian dies
Searchers find laugh tracks

—Jim Milstead

Applause, curtains. Now
Exit stage right, Become one's
Own understudy.

—Jim Milstead

winter rain . . .
the cemetery gate opened
for no one

—Lenard D. Moore, *Modern Haiku, 39.3*, 2008

Breathe in,
to the spring and my birth.

Breathe out,
to the summer of my youth.

Breathe in,
to the autumn of my life.

Breathe out,
to the winter of my death.

by Ron Moss

—Ron C. Moss, *DailyHaiga.org*, 2009

Robert Epstein

starry night
what's left of my life
is enough

—Ron C. Moss, *Shiki Internet Kukai Contest*, 2006

tired of this world...
suddenly moonlight
through my window

—Ron C. Moss, *Simply Haiku, 3:4*, 2005

autumn ends unable to explain what I've lost

—marlene mountain

brushing off sand
I walk what's left of
the pine dunes
my time here passes by
like the birds overhead

—Gene Murtha, *Ribbons 5:2,* 2009

down the hillpath
fallen leaves follow me
into the shadows

—Patricia Neubauer

all I could ask for
in summertime
just the snapping
of grass-hoppers
when I pass

—Peter Newton, *Modern English Tanka, 3: 1,* 2008

staring at the still life for what is a lifetime

—Peter Newton, *Modern Haiku, 36.1,* 2005

Time is teaching me
how to collapse
what can I say
it's been a long life
I could sleep for a week

—Peter Newton, *Modern English Tanka, 2: 3*, 2008

a small cloud
across the moon

a single print
in melting snow

soon

    —ayaz daryl nielsen

these death poems—
grandson hearing Bashō's
asks for mine

    —H. F. Noyes

on my dying bed
a neighbor boy reads out
the ball scores

    —H. F. Noyes

Robert Epstein

diagnosis —
spring sweeter
because of it

    —Marian Olson, *bottle rockets, #14*, 2006

ending
in wildflowers . . .
the logging road

    —Tom Painting, *South by Southeast, 5:3*, 1998

year's end
I give the graveyard
a passing glance

    —Tom Painting, *Frogpond, 33: 3*, 2010

my library filled
with books I hope to read
again
I fear I've planned
too far ahead

    —Kathe L. Palka, *red lights, 6:1*, 2010

braver today
after reading all those haiku
about death

   —Greg Pico, *Modern Haiku, 41.2,* 2010

death poem   maybe tomorrow

   —Jennifer Gomoll Popolis, *Modern Haiku, 41.2,* 2010

twilight deepens
the wordless things
I know

   —Francine Porad, *Tidepool, 8,* 1991

cruising
the back roads home
soft slow sunrise

   —Ellen Pratte

two river banks
one more pull to reach
the other one

   —Vera Primorac

Robert Epstein

this life . . .
a soap bubble beautiful
before it bursts

—Kala Ramesh, *bottle rockets, #15*, 2006

born to live I hoe
and, ah, born to die
i kiss the melon

—William R. Ramsey, *Modern Haiku, 40.3*, 2009

stupid mayflies
not knowing the start,
the end of things

—William R. Ramsey, *More Wine*, 2010

the light turning green
against a vast night—
my turn to go

—William R. Ramsey, *More Wine*, 2010

Dried lavender sprigs
Sustain continuing scent—
Death does not take all.

—David A. Reinstein, http://www.associatedcontent.com/article/
430814/death_does_not_take_all_a_haiku.html?cat=10, 2007

my body thinner these days I hear more of the wind

    —Chad Lee Robinson, *Frogpond 33:2*, 2010

Eschatalogy

While all your bowers
crisp in heat, gardener Christ,
have one more rose leap.

    —Raymond Roseliep, *A ROSELIEP RETROSPECTIVE*, 1980

ordering my tombstone:
the cutter has me feel
his Gothic "R"

    —Raymond Roseliep, *LISTEN TO LIGHT*, 1980

This time!
I am
A log in the fire

    —David Rosen

slow winter clouds
the slightest turning
of a prayer strip

    —Bruce Ross, *summer drizzles*, 2005

         Robert Epstein

without me
my shoes so still
on the floor

—Bruce Ross, *summer drizzles*, 2005

Eavesdropping
on the leaves
dropping.

—Alexis Rotella, *DailyHaiga.org*, 2009

yellow butterfly
takes off the meadow
    — I will be sky, too

    —Djurdja Vukelic-Rozic

an autumn walk
while crushing fallen leaves
I think of my bones

    —Djurdja Vukelic-Rozic

a still lake —
nothing to mirror
but the sky

    —Djurdja Vukelic-Rozic

rewriting my life
the final edit
delete

    —Tracy Royce

dying chaplain still unsure

    —Helen Russell, *Modern Haiku, 39.1,* 2008

Robert Epstein

dance haiku

1. Do we dance
   death in a fast lane
   of salsa

2. or minuet
   death with an aristocrat's
   pointed toe

3. do we ease
   into death with
   workingclass abandon

4. or position our
   legs in middleclass
   laughter

5. do we swallow
   death in a fast gulp
   of morning pills

6. or factor death
   into prime years
   in our throats?

   —Sonia Sanchez, *morning haiku*, 2010

winter solstice walk
out to the cliff . . .
wondering

   —Jusy Schattner

I've got death
on my lips
a final kiss

—Jay Schlesinger

lingering light—
the last of the coffee shared
this summer solstice
ware that tomorrow
will be a short day

—Adelaide Shaw, *Tanka Cafe, #6,* 2004

is there spring again
at the end of our winter
or is that a tale
spun of gossamer threads
to soothe the weary?

—Adelaide Shaw, *Red Lights,* 2008

TOCK

we're all here
on borrowed time
some just have
more ticks . . .

—Kevin Shaw, *The Uncovered Bridge,* 2009

Robert Epstein

CHARLIE BROWN

. . . we are
but a shelled
   peanut
at the bottom
 of the bag
  awaiting
 our turn . . .

—Kevin Shaw

All those multitudes
who died alone and silent.
Why do I feel joy?

—Edith Shiffert, *The Light Comes Slowly*, 1997

In a mountain field
I wait for death. An ox eats
flowers, licks my face.

—Edith Shiffert, *The Light Comes Slowly*, 1997

Before the great change
lie at ease upon the earth—
soon you will have it.

—Edith Shiffert, *The Light Comes Slowly*, 1997

The body of bliss
warms us before departure.
Is there still more light?

—Edith Shiffert, *The Light Comes Slowly*, 1997

a raindrop—
behind glass, old photos
of leaving

—Sherry Weaver Smith, *California Quarterly 35.3*, 2009

preparing for
my death
I sort the bills

—Carmi Soifer

hard-drive crash
I practice dying

—Carmi Soifer

I look outside
at the end of the day—
cherry blossoms

—Carmi Soifer

Robert Epstein

autumn passing
for me no gods
no buddhas

—Robert Spiess, *sticks and pebbles*, 2001

lethal injection
though first, an alcohol swab
to thwart infection

—Robert Spiess, *sticks and pebbles*, 2001

but then when i
    no longer ride [the bus]
will any say
    where is that guy
i sat beside
    the other day

—Robert Spiess, *sticks and pebbles*, 2001

obituary page . . .
my name not there
so I go to work

—Bett Angel-Stawarz, *Frogpond, 33:1*, 2010

so awkward
that stage between
birth & death

    —Art Stein, *Modern Haiku, 39.2,* 2008

my fervid wish
to predecease
my dog

    — Art Stein

not finishing
anything I start
  until now

    —Art Stein

when you hear
of my skyward release
gather outdoors
in the light of dawn
and sing a hymn of hope

    —Carmen Sterba, *Ribbons, 2:2,* 2006

Robert Epstein

However young I was
when I stopped wanting
to stay up all night,
I knew it as a step toward death,
and felt it as a relief.

 —John Stevenson, *The Tanka Anthology*, 2003

thought I was going somewhere March wind

 —John Stevenson, *Live Again*, 2009

seated between us
the imaginary
middle passenger

 —John Stevenson, *Live Again*, 2009

bringing in
some of the cold
when we enter
taking some of the warmth
when we depart

 —John Stevenson, *Live Again*, 2009

I put myself
in the shoes
of a dying friend.
He'd moved on by then
in his bare feet . . .

    —John Stevenson, *Ribbons, 1:4*, 2005

how do you feel about the rain   yesterday   today   tomorrow

    —Laurie W. Stoelting

this longing
    to go home . . .
white chrysanthemum

    —Ebba Story

twilight chill
closer than I thought
beauty & death

    —André Surridge

reminding me I am dust this shaft of sunlight

    —André Surridge

    Robert Epstein

last card how much of my life remains

   —André Surridge

against this
vast backdrop of eternity
the transience
of our little lives . . .
a firefly

   —André Surridge

a bug, a bullet
a breakdown of the heart
one way or other, we go—
the winter sunset has
a purple afterglow

   —George Swede, *bottle rockets, #20*, 2009

falling pine needles   the tick of the clock

   —George Swede, *Haiku Canada Newsletter, 3*, 1990

winter sunset
my shadow far too long
for one life

   —George Swede, *Joy in Me Still*, 2010

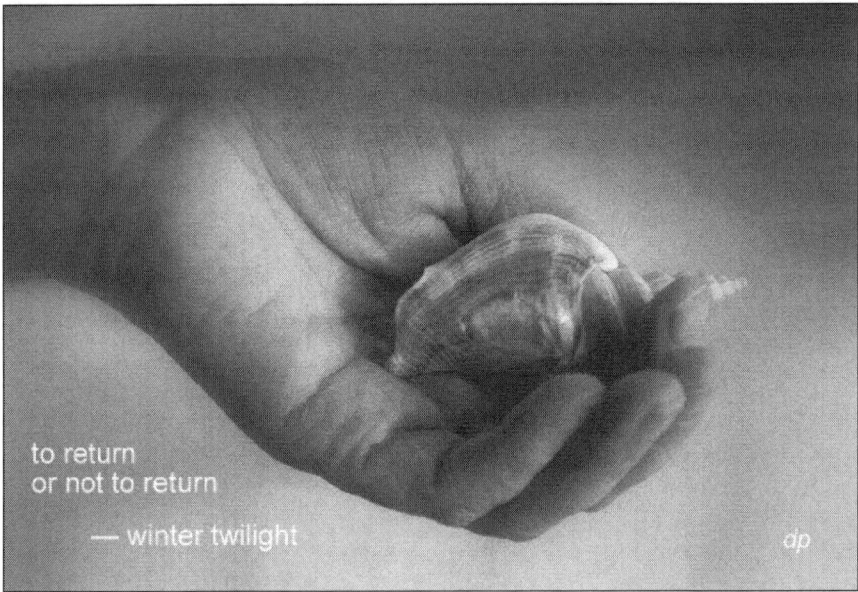

to return
or not to return

— winter twilight

dp

—Leszek Szeglowski
Dorota Pyra (Art), *DailyHaiga.org*, 2010

winter dusk
my shadow enters
the mirror

—Dietmar Tauchner

winter flu . . .
the trace of death
in the evening wind

—Dietmar Tauchner

at the abyss
at the abyss
lilac scent

—Dietmar Tauchner

all Soul's Eve
a strange face
in the mirror

—Dietmar Tauchner

his face reflected
in broken glass—
I hope I pass first

—Stacy Taylor

ting-ting
emptying
the rice bowl

—Carolyn Thomas, *Frogpond, 5:3*, 1982

come play with me
spring is
in the garden
and I must leave soon

—Marc Allen Thompson, *The Tanka Anthology*, 2003

waking to a chill
the calendar reads
Day of the Dead

 —Tony A. Thompson, *bottle rockets, #22,* 2010

     death

mirrors   circles

     life

 —Carrie Ann Thunell

sunrise
sunset—
the endless sky

 —Carrie Ann Thunell

five sheaths*
cocoon the soul
the endless journey

 —Carrie Ann Thunell

* The Hindu belief that a human consists of five sheaths, each more subtle than the last.
—Poet's note

          Robert Epstein

the birds are on wing,
the leaves fly in the wind
as I leave you.
   choose the flower you see
   from my life, and hold it close.

  —Doris Horton Thurston

it's a small favor
but scatter me well where
I have already lived

  —Doris Horton Thurston

"Ah . . ."
could be
a death poem

   vincent tripi, *bottle rockets #17*, 2007

The old pond
   my death poem
      plop!

  —vincent tripi

Death poem
    an exclamation pt.
        but in pencil

   —vincent tripi, *bottle rockets, #22*, 2010

the train whistle death poem the train

   —vincent tripi

Saved
   for my death poem
the firefly-jar

   —vincent tripi, *bottle rockets, #14*, 2006

the talk of the retirement home
death of an ornamental pine

   —Charles Trumbull

death watch:
boughs of the plum tree
in changeable winds

   —Charles Trumbull

                   Robert Epstein

playing hide and seek
in the shadows of gravestones —
the children

 —Charles Trumbull

ever longer nights:
driving back I feel smaller
than when I came

 —Charles Trumbull

sickbed solace:
a wall clock
with a broken minute hand

 —Charles Trumbull

from behind me
the shadow of the ticket-taker
comes down the aisle

 —Cor van den Heuvel, *Curbstones*, 1998

the shadow in the folded napkin

 —Cor van den Heuvel, *Curbstones*, 1998

a stick goes over the falls at sunset

 —Cor van den Heuvel, *Curbstones*, 1998

falling, a crimson leaf carried by the wind.
my life goes on . . . .

 —don vanvalkenburgh

the tenuous whistling
of the wind in the bottle
has come to an end

 —Max Verhart, *Woodpecker, 1*, 1995

under the shower
my bare feet remind me of
my mortality

 —Max Verhart

Pages of the book
next to the gone-out candle
turned by the wind now.

 —Sasa Vazic, *Ko*, 2005

     Robert Epstein

no
death
poem

— Karma Tenzing Wangchuk

waiting for me
to give it life—
my death poem

—Karma Tenzing Wangchuk

where this body will drop no matter

—Karma Tenzing Wangchuk, *Beachcomber*, 2000

my shadow ephemeral too

—Karma Tenzing Wangchuk, *Lilliput Review, #156*, 2007

in the end
just-as-I-am
will have to do

—Karma Tenzing Wangchuk, *Lilliput Review, #7*, 2003

imitating death
the 'possum' on his back
beneath the catawba tree
I sit and imagine
myself without a self

—Linda Jeannette Ward, *bottle rockets, #22*, 2010

Death
there all the time
like symphonies
in Beethoven's brain
a river cracking through ice

—Linda Jeannette Ward, *Haibun and Tanka Prose, 2*, 2009

death at my shoulder
every day now
I see more brightly
through the hollows
of the moon

—Linda Jeannette Ward, *Blithe Spirit*, 2008

like a prelude
to the final movement
all these little deaths
in lovemaking
emptiness becomes full

—Linda Jeannette Ward, *Ash Moon Anthology*, 2008

Robert Epstein

Fallow garden—
Stumps of moldering plants with
Tattered, shredded stalks.

   Kathy Waters

dental gold—
I will it to my son

   —Carmel Lively Westerman

party of one
whisky, water back
last call

   —Neal Whitman

every autumn
another year older . . .
half moon

   —Dick Whyte

first cicada . . .
how quickly I approach
my death

   —Dick Whyte

let death happen
on a spring morning
when dragonfly larvae
are crawling up the reeds
and drying in the sun

—Theresa Williams

End of summer
Just another thing
I can't hang on to

—Thom Williams, *Modern Haiku, 37.2*, 2006

football weather
I consider a codicil
to my will

—Billie Wilson, *Frogpond, 32:1*, 2009

numbered days
the black winter road
beyond our headlights

—Billie Wilson

Robert Epstein

Watch the sky.
You'll see
how long things last

    —Bill Zavatsky, *2010 Haiku Calendar*

Children jump the surf
waves shatter the summer air—
in a few years
friends will scatter my ashes
into such broken water.

    —J. Zimmerman, *Moonbathing, #1*, 2009

Storms this morning
keep me home recycling
inessential documents,
discarding yet again
all those people I once was.

    —J. Zimmerman, *Eucapypt, #4*, 2008

The falconer
raises her fist
this brief life

    —J. Zimmerman, *Flying White*, 2006

rising sun—
the sunflowers'
dark heads

—Verica Zivkovic

the shadows
of an abandoned station—
spring moon

—Verica Zivkovic

Suggested Reading

Anderson, P. ALL OF US: AMERICANS TALK ABOUT THE MEANING OF DEATH. NY: Delacorte Press, 1996.

Bastian, E. W. and Staley, T. L. LIVING FULLY DYING WELL: REFLECTING ON DEATH TO FIND YOUR LIFE'S MEANING. Boulder, CO: Sounds True, 2009.

Becker, C. B. BREAKING THE CIRCLE: DEATH AND THE AFTERLIFE IN BUDDHISM. IL: Southern Illinois University, 1993.

Berger, A. Practicing Death: Alternate Views. JOURNAL OF TRANSPERSONAL PSYCHOLOGY, 2010, 42:1, pp. 48-60.

Blackman, S. GRACEFUL EXITS: HOW GREAT BEINGS DIE. Boston: Shambhala, 2005.

Critchey, S. THE BOOK OF DEAD PHILOSOPHERS. NY: Vintage, 2008.

Dass, R. STILL HERE: EMBRACING AGING, CHANGING AND DYING. NY: Riverhead Books, 2000.

Dimidjian, V. J. JOURNEYING EAST: CONVERSATIONS ON AGING AND DYING. Berkeley, CA: Parallax Press, 2004.

Fenwick, P. and Fenwick, E. THE ART OF DYING: A JOURNEY TO ELSEWHERE. NY: Continuum, 2008.

Franke, R. American Death Poems. Blithe Spirit, Vol. 17, No. 1, March, 2007.

Grayson, D. The Ancient Enemy: Death in Art and Haiku. Modern Haiku, 41.1, Winter-Spring, 2010.

Halifax, J. BEING WITH DYING: Boston: Shambhala, 2009.

Hanh, T. N. NO DEATH, NO FEAR. NY: Riverhead, 2002.

Harrison, S. THE LOVE OF UNCERTAINTY. Boulder, CO: Sentient Publications, 2008.

Hoffmann, Y, ed. JAPANESE DEATH POEMS. Rutland, VT: Charles E. Tuttle, 1986.

Krishnamurti, J. THE BOOK OF LIFE: DAILY MEDITATIONS WITH KRISHNAMURTI. San Francisco: HarperSanFrancisco, 1995.

_____. THE FIRST AND LAST FREEDOM: Wheaton, IL: Quest Books, 1954.

_____. ON LIVING AND DYING. Sandpoint, ID: Morning Light Press, 2005.

_____. THE POCKET KRISHNAMURTI. Boston: Shambhala. 2009.

Kübler-Ross, E. ON DEATH AND DYING. New York, NY: Scribners, 2003.

_____. THE WHEEL OF LIFE. New York, NY: Simon & Schuster, 1997.

Loy, D.. LACK AND TRANSCENDENCE: THE PROBLEM LIFE AND DEATH IN PSYCHOTHERAPY, EXISTENTIALISM, AND BUDDHISM. Amherst, NY: Humanity Books, 2000.

Levine, S. A YEAR TO LIVE. NY: Bell Tower, 1997.

_____. HEALING INTO LIFE AND DEATH. NY: Anchor, 1987.

_____. WHO DIES? NY: Anchor, 1982.

Phillipe, A. THE HOUR OF OUR DEATH. Hamondsworth: Penguin, 1981.

Rilke, R. LETTERS ON LIFE. U. Baer, tr. NY. Modern Library. 2005.

Rosenberg, L. with Guy, D. LIVING IN THE LIGHT OF DEATH: ON THE ART OF BEING TRULY ALIVE. Boston: Shambhala, 2000.

Sogyal Rinpoche, THE TIBETAN BOOK OF LIVING AND DYING. Gafney, P. and Harvey, A., eds. San Francisco: HarperSanFrancisco, 1994.

Suzuki, S. ZEN MIND, BEGINNER'S MIND. NY: Weatherhill, 1970.

Vargas, J. B. THE PROMISE OF DEATH AND THE PASSION OF LIFE: A REFLECTIVE EXPLORATION OF DEATH, LOSS, AND LIVING FULLY. Rancho Cucamongo, CA. Luminary Enterprises, 2005.

Yalom, I. STARING AT THE SUN: OVERCOMING THE TERROR OF DEATH. San Francisco: Jossey-Bass, 2008.

About the Editor

Robert Epstein is a psychotherapist and haiku poet living in the San Francisco Bay Area. His poetry has appeared in *Acorn, bottle rockets, Frogpond, The Heron's Nest, Mariposa, Modern Haiku, moonset, South by Southeast,* and other publications. An anthology, *THE BREATH OF SURRENDER: A COLLECTION OF RECOVERY-ORIENTED HAIKU,* was published in 2009 by the Modern English Tanka Press. Robert is currently at work on a book of his own death awareness poems entitled, *CHECK OUT TIME IS NOON: A YEAR OF DEATH AWARENESS HAIKU.*

Death Awareness Blog

Please consider visiting the blog on death awareness poetry that Robert has launched, DREAMS WANDER ON, where you can share your reflections on death and mortality, or post a haiku, senryu, or tanka on the theme of death awareness. The DREAMS WANDER ON blog may be accessed at: deathawarenesshaiku.blogspot.com

Also from MODERN ENGLISH TANKA PRESS

First Winter Rain: Selected Tanka from 2000–2006 - Denis M. Garrison

Take Five: Best Contemporary Tanka, Volume Two ~ M. Kei, Sanford Goldstein, Patricia Prime, Kala Ramesh, Alexis Rotella, Angela Leuck, Eds.

Double Take: Response Tanka ~ Sonja Arntzen and Naomi Beth Wakan.

Home to Ballygunge: Kolkata Tanka ~ William Hart

Black Jack Judy and the Crisco Kids: Bronx Memories ~ Tanka by Alexis Rotella

Where We Go: haiku and tanka sequences and other concise imaginings by Jean LeBlanc.

The Time of This World: 100 tanka from 13 collections by Kawano Yuko, trans. Amelia Fielden & Saeko Ogi.

Peeling an Orange ~ Haiku by Peggy Heinrich. Photographs by John Bolivar.

A Breath of Surrender: A Collection of Recovery-Oriented Haiku ~ Robert Epstein, Ed.

A Poetic Guide to an Ancient Capital: Aizu Yaichi and the City of Nara ~ Michael F. Marra

Elvis In Black Leather ~ Tanka by Alexis Rotella

The Stream Singing Your Name ~ Tanka and Sijo by Jean LeBlanc

Streetlights: Poetry of Urban Life in Modern English Tanka ~ Michael McClintock & Denis M. Garrison, Eds..

Take Five: Best Contemporary Tanka ~ Anthology. M. Kei, Sanford Goldstein, Pamela A. Babusci, Patricia Prime, Bob Lucky & Kala Ramesh, Eds.

All the Horses of Heaven ~ Tanka by James Tipton

Tanka from the Edge ~ Miriam Sagan

Jack Fruit Moon ~ Robert D. Wilson

Meals at Midnight ~ Poems by Michael McClintock

Lilacs After Winter ~ Francis Masat

Proposing to the Woman in the Rear View Mirror ~ Haiku & Senryu by James Tipton.

Looking for a Prince: a collection of senryu and kyoka ~ Alexis Rotella

The Tanka Prose Anthology ~ Jeffrey Woodward, Ed.

Greetings from Luna Park ~ Sedoka, James R. Burns

In Two Minds ~ Responsive Tanka by Amelia Fielden and Kathy Kituai

An Unknown Road ~ Haiku by Adelaide B. Shaw

Ash Moon Anthology: Poems on Aging in Mod. Engl. Tanka ~ Alexis Rotella & Denis M. Garrison, Eds.

Fire Blossoms: The Birth of Haiku Noir ~ haiku noirs by Denis M. Garrison

Sailor in the Rain and Other Poems ~ free and formal verse by Denis M. Garrison

Four Decades on My Tanka Road ~ Sanford Goldstein. Fran Witham, Ed.

Jun Fujita, Tanka Pioneer ~ Denis M. Garrison, Ed.

Landfall: Poetry of Place in Mod. English Tanka ~ Denis M. Garrison and Michael McClintock, Eds.

Lip Prints: Tanka . . . 1979-2007 ~ Alexis Rotella

Ouch: Senryu That Bite ~ Alexis Rotella

Eavesdropping: Seasonal Haiku ~ Alexis Rotella

Five Lines Down: A Landmark in English Tanka ~ Denis M. Garrison, Ed.

Tanka Teachers Guide ~ Denis M. Garrison, Ed.

Sixty Sunflowers: TSA Members' Anthology 2006-2007 ~ Sanford Goldstein, Ed.

The Dreaming Room: Mod. Engl. Tanka in Collage & Montage Sets ~ M. McClintock & D.M. Garrison, Eds.

The Salesman's Shoes ~ Tanka, James Roderick Burns

Hidden River ~ Haiku by Denis M. Garrison

The Five-Hole Flute: Mod. Engl. Tanka in Sequences & Sets ~ D.M. Garrison & M. McClintock, Eds.